AUTUMN LEAVES:

The Seasons of Life

William C. Moore, Jr.

Copyright © 2007 by William C. Moore, Jr.

All rights reserved. No part of this book may be reproduced or transmitted in any form or by any means without permission by the author.

Library of Congress Cataloging-in-Publication Data available

ISBN 978-0-6151-6911-8

Table of Contents

SPRING 1
   A Broomstick Pony Named Apple 2
   A Walk in Grandmother's Garden 3
   Butterfly 5
   Childhood 6
   Fidus Achates 7
   Four Queens and a King 8
   Fun in the Sun 9
   Halloween 10
   Heroes in No One's Eyes 11
   Holiday Time 13
   If 14
   In Praise of Spring 15
   MOTHER 16
   On All Hallows Eve 17
   Plain Country Cooking 18
   Spring 20
   Stranger on a Steel Gray Horse 21
   Summers at Uncle Joe's 23
   Tears of Lady Spring 24
   The Place of Childhood Dreams 25
   The Silver Sea Shell Box 26
   Waiting for Spring 28
Summer 29
   A Moment of Madness 30
   A Walk in a Forest Glade 31
   Advice to a Young Man 33
   Alone With My Thoughts 34
   An Angel Flew By My Window 35
   An Angry Lady 36
   Coffee 38
   Contemplation 39
   Does the Soul Cry Out? 40

Dreams of Absurdity 41
Enlightenment 42
Eulogy to an Unknown Man 44
Family Man. 45
First Kiss, Last Memory 46
Fishing with Dad. 48
Flapper. 50
For Tom 51
For Trish: Let the Party Begin 53
From Babylon-By-The-Sea 54
Hath Thee No Love For Me, My Lady? 55
I Beheld Thee in a Dream. 57
I Sit In Contemplation 58
Morning 59
Autumn 61
It's Autumn 62
Like Sweet Love Always 63
Lines On A Map 64
Man and Hurricane. 65
Mankind 66
Missing You 68
Mornings by the Sea 69
My Beloved. 71
My Love 72
New Orleans, The Queen City .73
Ode to a Country Road 75
Ode to a Summer Morning 76
Perchance We Should Meet Someday. 78
Playing Life's Game 79
Sitting by the Ocean 80
The Ballad of Paris Parker 81
The Devil's Gold Mine 83
The Journal 85
The Killing of Rebecca 86
The Sailor 87

    The Visit 88
    The Whispering Winds 91
    The Writer's Struggle 92
    Tread Carefully, O Man 93
    Upon Leaving the Company of Friends. 94
    Windows. 95
    You Can't Hold Me Back 96
Winter. 99
    Awakening to a New Day. 100
    Birthday Boy 101
    Capturing the Moment 102
    Choices, Paths and Trails 103
    Daffodil Hill. 105
    Dare To Be 106
    Day Has Gently Closed the Door 107
    For Winter is Drawing Neigh 109
    Home to Bellevue 111
    Images of Life 112
    Judgment Day 113
    Make Gentle the Ride Across the River 114
    Memories 115
    Memories of an Icy Winter 116
    Missing Yesterday 118
    Musings on a Lifetime. 119
    Night 121
    Old Age and I. 122
    Old Age and Memories 123
    On the Way to Eternity 125
    Reflections on Aging. 126
    So Soft the Winds of Yesterday 128
    The Path of Life. 129
    The Snows of Yesteryear 130
    Then The Winter Came 131
    Thoughts on a Foggy Day 132
    To Hear the Wild Birds Sing 133

When Judging Others 134

SPRING

William C. Moore, Jr.

A Broomstick Pony Named Apple

What days those were so long ago
Carefree, relaxing and fun. Just me
And a broomstick pony named Apple
Exploring a brave new world
In a childhood hide-a-way place.

At Hilltop Point I could look all around
Taking in my beautiful world.
Green Meadows below me all quiet and still,
The slopes were covered with oaks and pines,
As I stood surveying from my hill.

Days filled with adventures and play
Where the hills and woods were all mine.
I went tearing through on a broomstick horse,
Chasing things that little boys chase,
In my childhood hide-a-way place.

Now I steal away to a place in my mind,
Away from the maddening crowds,
Where time and no man can dwell.
Back to the place where I was a child,
A place I remember so well.

The woods and meadow still look the same
But the little boy's all grown up.
I linger for a while looking out from the hill
Searching for the boy and a broomstick pony
That went by the name of Apple.

AUTUMN LEAVES:

A Walk in Grandmother's Garden

Yesterday I passed a flower vendor
Her cart was overflowing
With cascading bouquets of color
Whose sweet clean fragrance filled the air
Bringing back memories of yesteryear
When I walked in Grandmother's garden.

Her garden was a special place
It filled a child with wonder
To see the creatures cut and shaped
From bushes, vines and flowers.
What an adventure it was
On a walk through Grandmother's garden.

A hedge of yew, all neatly trimmed
Enclosed this curious place
Where a laurel bear danced amongst the iris
And a boxwood seal balanced a ball of petunias
On a walk through Grandmother's garden.

Down by the pool a fish was swimming
in a sea of yellow daffodils
While a frog sat admiring his reflection
From a chair of marigolds.
What glorious things there were to see
On a walk through Grandmother's garden.

Amongst the foxgloves sat a santolina rabbit
Hiding from an ivy owl perched up on an ancient column
A butterfly bed of pansies fluttered near the roses.

William C. Moore, Jr.

From a peach tree trellis swung a jasmine hummingbird.
What exciting creatures you could see
On a walk through Grandmother's garden.

I would go back to that place again
If time would but allow it.
Go back and live those lovely days
On a walk through Grandmother's garden.

AUTUMN LEAVES:

Butterfly

A Summer's morning, a field of yellow
A walk on a winding path
The world is bright and I'm so mellow
Flutter by, Butterfly.

An Autumn evening the air is still
The world is holding its breath
For the coolness of the daily chill
Flutter by, Butterfly.

Winter's day, the cold winds blow
The rains sound just like a drum,
To the east there's ten feet of snow
Now there's no Butterfly to flutter by.

At last the Spring, the warming touch,
The flowers have started to bloom.
A joyful season we missed so much
Do flutter by, Butterfly

Childhood

The day has awakened in all its glory.
Gone is the gray fog of last night's sleep.
Arise, O Sun, and give us warmth,
Free all things from night's cold darkness.
Call forth the birds to fill the sky
And permeate the air with song.
Let loose the insects to buzz and hum amongst
The trees and flowers.
Open each blossom and perfume the air
With Nature's secret fragrance.
Release the child in every man to
Play in youthful wonder.
Return those long forgotten years
Of cowboys, knights and pirates
When dreams were real and reality
Was, but dreams in the dark of night.
Bring back in all children of light
The gift of eternal childhood.

Fidus Achates

"fE-dus-a-'ka-tAs"
faithful Achates: Trusted Friend

You are my faithful friend whom I call brother.
My companion when times are filled with doubt
And life is long, fill with dread and fear.
You lift your glass in salute to banish despair
Leading me from myself into the sunlight.
My Fidus Achates, my friend, my brother,
With you in my life there is joy and hope.

William C. Moore, Jr.

Four Queens and a King

There are four queens and a king in my royal court.
Playmates from childhood, friends everlasting.
Squabbles, fights and laughing support
A wonderful job of casting.

My sisters are a brilliant blend.
Joy, beauty, truth and love sprinkled heavily with wit.
Laughter reigns around them ever without end,
To a joyous, happy life they did commit.

The king, my brother, is a wise and noble man.
Strong, brave and stalwart is this brother mine.
He is the patient, loving brother of this clan.
What he means to me I never can define.

I'm now in the sunset years of life
And looking back on my childhood
Fills me with great delight.
My sister and my brother are the joys of my boyhood.

Though we've grown old and are past our prime.
Memories are forever young.
The years haven't always been kind,
But it's a wonderful life's song that we've sung.

Fun in the Sun

I wake up with the rising sun
Eager to start a new day.
There are list of things that must be done
And things I can do to play.
Time puts its stamp on each day
We are ruled by hours and minutes.
This many hours for working
And these few hours for play.
I want to revolt and just run away
I'm tired of the work routine.
Where are the fun things that I want to do
When the day is filled with working?
Never ending list that must be done
Before I can go have some fun.
I tackle the list, check them off as they're done,
As the day wears on and on, all day long
I'm still at home doing the jobs that aren't any fun.
I spend a few minutes sipping a coffee
Planning my day in the sun.
It's back on the job to get the work done
Then I sit and rest for a while.
The sun's come and gone, I've worked all day long
Never once getting outside for some sun.
Tomorrow's a new day I'll while the time away
Go out and take a run.
But a new list has started as daylight departed
I'll just work on it out in the sun...tomorrow.

William C. Moore, Jr.

Halloween

With faces cut and carved on each
The pumpkins line the steps.
Inside a candle burns so bright
For it is Halloween tonight.
Spiders play in their webs,
While bats fly overhead,
A witch gives out treats to all
That comes knocking on her door.
"Come in, come in, my pretty,
Let's see what I have for you.
Some spiders are nice, they wiggle
And squirm as you chew off all their legs.
The bats are excellent this time of year
I think I'll give you two.
Oh, and here's a big black scary cat
That's filled with marshmallow goo.
You must take some pumpkin heads
They're really good for you.
Goodbye, goodbye, I really must fly."
She grabbed her broom and closed the door
On another Halloween.

AUTUMN LEAVES:

Heroes in No One's Eyes

Late May and the weather is hot and humid
Just like it was when I left all those years ago.
Things have changed to newer, bigger and brighter,
But the people have remained untouched.
Kind, friendly, "Glad to see you back."
"How long will you stay this time?"
"Ya'll drop in for some coffee and cake."
"I saw your brother the other day..."
Genuine interest in the things that make
Up your life's story.
It's all about the caring and love
They hold for all your family.
Everyone in the village is part of your
Childhood, an extended family.
They don't change, they let the world
Around them change and
Merely adapt it to their lives.
Wonderful people are these,
Friends and neighbors since birth.
Schoolmates content to stay put
And live the life of their forefathers.
To those who have been struck by
Wanderlust, they talk of days of
Quiet perfection when the world was
Innocent as were we.
Day in the park, playing, swimming,
The joyous days of summer,
The innocence of youth.
These little pockets of humanity
Go about life with joy and purpose.

William C. Moore, Jr.

They tend their gardens and mind their own affairs.
Always ready to help their neighbors
In whatever way they can.
All of the children had the experience
Of every grown up for guidance and help.
They were heroes in no one's eyes,
But heroes all the same.

AUTUMN LEAVES:

Holiday Time

Polish the silver, wash all the crystal,
Get out the very best china,
Put down the damask on the long dining table
For it is holiday time once again.

Gather the family, call all the friends,
There's always room for one more.
Decorate the door and dust all the rooms
Then let the party begin.

Bring out the turkey, all golden brown,
Filled with stuffing just right,
Set down the platters and bowls
Each filled to the top with good cheer.

Let's eat, drink and be merry all night
For love and good friends abound.
We'll talk of the good times and good dinners
We've had and laugh all night long.

At long last when the party winds down
And the toddlers keep nodding their heads
We'll dress them up warmly, kiss each one gently,
Then carry then home and to bed.

If

If I could make each day Spring
If I could make the flowers sing
If I could part the seven seas
If I could fly with the birds and bees
If I could, would I?

If life was like a fairy tale
If only goodness did prevail
If all bad things were turned to dust
If men didn't fight the unjust
If they could, would they?

If yesterday was now anew
If we could go back and review
If things could turn out differently
If life would go on triumphantly
If life could, would it?

If youth and age could both agree
If maturity could issue a decree
If every day was not a test
If all our day are truly blessed
If we could, would we?

In Praise of Spring

When listening to the rain falling down
For what seem like a thousand years
Life seems to be a sad, sad clown
Shedding cold clear crystal tears.

While waiting for the sun to shine
Just keep your fingers crossed
The glory of the sun divine
Will not on man be lost.

Just feel the softly blowing breeze
That gently whispers your name
For the soul it does appease
And the joy of Spring proclaim.

Awake the world in proclamation
Life has begun anew
Time has come for celebration
For Winter is now through.

William C. Moore, Jr.

MOTHER

Made from the stardust of heaven above.
Often called an angel by all. A
Tender, loving gentle and kind
Heart of every family.
Each child treated as if they're the only one.
Reaching beyond all boundaries as love incarnate.

On All Hallows Eve

The sounds of laughter echoes in the halls
The voices of children playing still vibrate in the walls
Footfalls run down the stairs, the front door closes with a bang,
From time long gone these shadows sprang
And carry on their living.

Behind the upstairs windows lace occasionally there is a face
That looks out into eternal space.
As they move about their world in phantom candle light
The Other Worlders stay away in dreadful scary fright
And carry on their living.

On All Hallows Eve they brave the dark
And come to the old house on a lark.
Bravely they enter through the door
Then are seen never more
And carry on their living.

William C. Moore, Jr.

Plain Country Cooking

My Mom was the greatest cook
In the old country tradition.
Plain and hardy, the country way
Her meals were a taste of heaven.
She had learned to cook
When she was a child
Just big enough to wear an apron.

The smells from her kitchen
Would soon fill the house
With the visions of dinner that night.
Southern fried chicken, mashed potatoes and gravy,
A tossed green salad with biscuits she made by hand.
Plenty of tea that was sweet and cold
And her famous banana pudding.

The wonderful aroma would bring us all in
So we could breathe all the love she put in that meal.
Quickly we would set up the table
And try not to get in her way.
When all was completed the first things she'd say is
"Go get your father, dinner is ready."
My sister would lead him back by the hand.

All through my youth I remember these meals
And how sadly they're missing today.
It's a frozen pizza or a take out dinner
From some chain of fast food diners
That feed the children these days.
I sit and I wonder just where it went

AUTUMN LEAVES:

The plain country cooking I knew.

William C. Moore, Jr.

Spring

At last the Winter months have passed
Those frigid nights, those dark cold days.
The sun now sits higher in the clear blue sky.
Breezes from the south now tempt the senses
With fragrances swept away from the islands.
Color sweeps across the land in patchwork pieces.
The brown of newly furrowed soil striped with green
As new grass thrust up from the long dead stubble.
How joyful is this day, how sweet the birds do sing.
All nature releases a sigh of thanksgiving
That once again it's Spring.

AUTUMN LEAVES:

Stranger on a Steel Gray Horse

Up passed the graveyard on Knobby Vine Road,
Down through Cold Mans Creek,
Over the hills to the Mounds of Goads,
Around the Oaks of Old Men,
Out of the black night astride a steel gray horse
Came calling a stranger in Marlborough Town.
The night was all misty, the moon bright and full
The trees cast black shadows upon the cold ground.
Don't answer the door if the stranger does knock.
Keep a candle in the windows and a lock on the doors.
Houses full of laughter for block after block,
But outside the cold winds does blow.
Misty shadows from long, long ago
Walk the quiet streets in phosphorescent glow.
The night is filled with witches on brooms
As the bats fly round and round.
The town hall bells strikes the sound of doom
When the stranger comes calling in Marlborough Town.

Cries and moans from the house on the hill
Long empty of human habitation.
Growls and groans have filled the night,
There are shrieks from the old train station,
When the stranger comes calling in Marlborough Town.
Beware, beware, this stranger, astride a steel gray horse
That comes calling in the dark of night.
Ill winds blow down leaf littered streets
Branches tap on windows till early morning light.
Cats of all colors will hiss, mew and growl
Dogs will howl and cower in fright.

William C. Moore, Jr.

Beware, beware, the cold winds do whisper
When out of the night astride his steel gray horse
Comes calling a stranger in Marlborough Town.
Who is this stranger that calls up this force
Moving silently over the course?
It's the Gatherer of Souls who comes this night
Sitting astride his steel gray horse.

Summers at Uncle Joe's

Tires singing as they touch the hot Summer asphalt
Excitement, expectations abound for the trip to Uncle Joe's.
What adventures would we have this year?
Where would our journey take us?
Down to the swimming hole at the cold creek,
Playing in the hay loft, swinging on the ropes,
Mucking out the stables, riding Bess and Bob,
Hiking to the general store to pick up needed supplies.

Fresh cold water straight from the well
Taking away our thirst.
Uncle Joe smelling of wood smoke and hard work
Telling dry humor jokes as we try to understand.
Picking peas, beans and tomatoes from out the side garden
Fresh bread baking for dinner tonight.

Children free to run about shoeless and shirtless
Sitting in the front porch swing while the grown-ups
Talk in private.
Sleep slowly creeping over us as cicadas softly call out
Dreams of playing, running and jumping with abandon
Starry nights, warm southern breezes, paradise for children.

Tears of Lady Spring

"Don't weep for me." said Father Winter to Lady Spring,
But Spring's sweet tears ran in rivulets down winding streets.
Wet gray clouds hang laden over the mountain crest
Touching tree tops to stay anchored as the wind blows in.
All to no avail as they are shaken loose by the fury.
She dries her eyes for a little while, but the sadness comes again.
All day her tears fall on this the first day of Spring.
Father Winter gives one last cough freezing her tears
Into soft pellets that fall clattering onto rooftops.
Sometimes soon the skies will turn blue as the sun comes out
From hiding to warm the earth so recently watered by Lady Spring.
Flowers will slowly cover the ground, blossoms will perfume the air
And the sadness of losing Father Winter will fade into yesterday.
When Lady Spring has come into her own.

The Place of Childhood Dreams

I remember your hills all covered in pines
Your streams running clear, deep and cold
Do you remember me?

Meadows green, lush with flowers pale
Crisscrossed with hidden trails
I remember your hills all covered in pines.

The smell of summer hanging heavy
The sound of wind through the trees
Do you remember me?

The long country road going nowhere
Dust clouds when cars raced by
I remember your hills all covered in pines.

I stand at the edge of the hilltop
And take in the lay of the land
Do you remember me?

Beautiful place of peace and joy
The place of childhood dreams
I remember your hills all covered in pines
Do you remember me?

The Silver Sea Shell Box

It set on Mother's vanity
For over fifty years
Polished each week for eternity
Washed clean with all her tears.

She held the box with loving hands
Taking care that it didn't fall
Gently then she set it back upon its silver stand
And chased the children into the hall.

The contents were for her alone
Not meant for other eyes to see
Time for that when she was gone
But for now she wore the key.

The treasures she so lovingly held
Within her sea shell box
Over the course of years did swell
But never did it break the lock.

The children begged and pleaded
For one glimpse into the shell
Tears and cries went unheeded
Upon deaf ears they fell.

We all grew up and moved away
But Mother kept her peace
Her silver sea shell box held sway
The begging would never cease.

AUTUMN LEAVES:

One sunny day she did cross over
With a smile upon her face
To tread forever upon emerald clover
In that beautiful heavenly place.

Her precious silver sea shell box
Sat on her vanity
On a pale blue card she had written in black
"Now you can open me."

At last the children were free to see
The secrets of the shell
Slowly the eldest turned the key
Nothing could break this spell.

The lid popped open like a spring trap
Pictures and letters came sliding out
All the children with their mouths agape
Knew at last what Mother's treasure was about.

William C. Moore, Jr.

Waiting for Spring

How quiet the night, how cold and still.
A million stars sparkle on snow covered ground
From the light of a distant moon.
High in the hills the call of a wolf
Rides the frigid night air clear and long.
Below in the valley smoke rises softly
From the cabin deep in white powder.
Under the ice covered stream the water
Complains at being denied the night skies.
Occasionally the hoot of a hunting owl drifts
Over the valley like wind blown snow.

For now life is slowed by Nature's cold sleep.
Days will click by one by one,
Until a warming breeze will fan the awakening
Of all the sleeping residents hidden below.
As sweet blood climbs up the tallest trees
Buds of beauty will cover each branch.
Soon through the melting snow sprouts of green
Will emerge to give the world bright colors
And the perfume of a thousand flowers.
Birds will fill the air with song
Happy that spring is here at last.

Summer

William C. Moore, Jr.

A Moment of Madness

The world constantly calls with inconstant rhythm
Of never ending streams of glitter and litter.
Screeching of tires, honking of horns, shouting out
The car window to the jerk that just cut you off.
But where is there a quiet place away from
The incessant hum of dreary little lives waiting
For fulfillment. They go weaving and bobbing through
Life like a rubber duck in a bathtub with promises of riches
On a ship that never come to port. Dime store
Blondes selling their lives as they try to reach their
Dreams of upper class stations. Slick haired gigolos
With bad breath hitting on the ladies as they walk
Down the street of dreams hoping to hit it lucky.
Only the Grandmothers and Grandfathers face life
With expectations of a new and joyful day while
The youngsters look for handouts to success and prosperity.
Perhaps it's time to join the man on the corner shouting
In madness and frustration that the end of the world is near.
I stop, listen and move on for I've had my moment of madness.

AUTUMN LEAVES:

A Walk in a Forest Glade

Surrounded by shades of green,
Feeling the coolness provided by
The canopy of leaves, I slowly
Wander through these verdant hills.
Time slows down and all noise
Is replaced by the crunch of dry
Leaves and the cracking of twigs.
All senses are heightened so
That the smallest of changes
Seem to be expanded.
Over there, by that rotting tree,
Grows a community of mushrooms
Intent on devouring all of it.
Inside the hollowed trunk
Hides a snake resting until night
So it can go in search of a meal.
By the stream a doe stands
Listening for any movement before
She takes a drink to assuage
Her thirst. She is all beauty and
Grace as she moves quietly
Through the trees.
Listen carefully and you can hear
The rustle of leaves made by
Some creature going about
Its daily routine of finding food.
Further down the trail a frog
Sits boldly on a stump croaking
To his lady love hiding somewhere
In the undergrowth.

William C. Moore, Jr.

Birds flit about in the trees
Singing and calling to friends.
Others are busy finding food
For their babies.
Squirrels, the acrobats of the forest,
Run up the trees as if they had wings
On their feet. Pausing momentarily
To survey the scene around them,
Ready to dash away from a hawk or
Any other being intent on making a
Meal of them, then scurry on
Toward their nest for a short nap.
A rabbit munches contentedly on
Fresh tender green leaves but is
Always on the alert for an intruder.
Carefully I walk within a few feet of it.
Am I really unnoticed or is this little
Gray bunny so confident that it can get
Away that it feels no need to run?
Perhaps it knows I mean it no harm and
Only want to enjoy its beauty.
At last, I've walked to the end of the trail
Before me lies the pasture where I can see
The setting sun. I leave the serene world
Of the glade and return to the world outside,
Leaving it as I found it undisturbed
And at peace.

Advice to a Young Man

Walk softly, young prince,
Lest thy ways bring trouble
Upon thy noble head. For love
Is not to be played as
One does a game of chance.
The heart of the fair maiden can be
Shattered by callous youth
And love can quickly sour into hate.

Whisper not words of love if
Only lust lies in thy heart for
Yon fair maiden believes thy
Words are true. Long will thee
Regret thy foolish impulse
To play games with Cupid's bow,
For surely will thy aim go
Astray and wound thyself.

Take heed, young prince, that
The dart thee sends isn't plucked
Out and sent back to thee by a
Knowing young maiden well versed
In the strategies of love and life.
If care is not given then thee will pay
The price for callousness as thy heart
Will be trampled underfoot and broken.

Alone With My Thoughts

Night has come and I'm alone with my thoughts
I sit still and watch them drift by.
A tiny wave upon the sea
Of constant moving images
Disrupts the pattern and flow
With a gently undulating swell.
The images merge and spin about
In a kaleidoscopic jumble
Old images turn into new images
Which turn into new images.
I sit still and watch them drift by.

An Angel Flew By My Window

An angel flew by my window,
But she didn't have time to stop.
She promised a child she would come by
Before she was carried home.
She held the child and made her smile
By telling her wonderful stories.

An angel flew by my window
On the way to a neighbor's house.
He had been sick for so very long
And was feeling so despondent.
She opened the blinds and let in the sun
Then sat there holding his hand.

An angel flew by my window
As she moved about on her duties.
Here she stopped to pick some flowers
To take to a soldier's sad mother.
Then wiped the tears from sad, sad eyes
Of the child without a home.

An angel flew by my window
With a smile she stopped for a moment.
My sorrow vanished in the bright cheery look
As she reached out and touched my cheek.
"Peace be with you this beautiful day."
She then went along on her way.

William C. Moore, Jr.

An Angry Lady

The hurricane is fast approaching
Just look up at the skies.
All the clouds are dark and brooding
Tears fall from their eyes.
Listen to the wind howling
As it's pitch climbs ever higher.
I should have know about this lady
Before so far from home I roamed.

I could have turned the TV on
To check up on the world,
But my studies are more important
Than to waste the time on bull.
I pray my home doesn't blow away
Because of this angry lady.
I can make it to my sister's house
She's just four blocks away.

It's three o'clock in the afternoon
But darkness has settled in.
The rain is heavy with determination
Sending the wind to free the course.
The porch is awash in soft green paste
From leaves pushed through the wire mesh.
This sad angry lady has arrived
Bent on total destruction.

The lights are out, there's no telephone,
But a quick check outside reveals
That lines are flailing like snakes in the air

AUTUMN LEAVES:

Popping, crackling, sparking heard above the howling storm.
A car creeps slowly down the street driven by the wind
Until at last it's stopped in the clutches of a gasping, shaking tree.
The streets have long since disappeared under a raging river.
Oh, Lord, hear our prayers.

Suddenly all is quiet.
No longer do the cruel winds blow.
No more the pelting rain.
It's the eye and peace will reign for just a little while.
With great care we go outside to survey the scary scene.
Signs have fallen from up the street.
The roof is gone from next door,
But the family is unscathed.

Before very long the wind picks up
It's from the other way.
Here comes the rain prepare for the worst
As the howling becomes a roar.
The house begins to quiver and shake
As once again the storm erupts.
We're huddled in the darkened room
Like mice afraid of the cat.

There's a booming crash against the house
As debris is hurled about.
Followed by a second thud,
But the windows remain intact.
After a few eternities of waiting for the end
The lady slowly lifts her skirts to go her blustery way,
Moving on to the north and flooding Tennessee.
Leaving behind one grateful and very scared family.

Coffee

From the darkness of the night
Rubbing sleep from my eyes
I fumble with the coffee maker
To fix my morning wake up.
The cat throws herself against my legs
Demanding her morning scratch
Before she'll eat her daybreak meal
And tell me about her night.
Ah, the coffee's perked.
Its last hiccup is proof that all is ready.
Now fill the cup and sip it slowly
To wash away the night.
Just one more cup to hype me up
And get the forces going.
Quickly shower, shave and pull on clothes
Then hit the door running
For God has made a perfect day
And there's just on time for grumbling.

AUTUMN LEAVES:

Contemplation

I sit in contemplation on the beauty of this world
I listen as the wind sings me a sad, sad song of love
I watch as leaves go dancing by dressed in Autumn colors
I see the birds in jovial groups departing for the winter
For soon the cold, cold snow and ice will cover everything
And life will slowly go to sleep for oh, the long, long night.

Sit thee in contemplation of soft this lovely spring
Let thine eye behold the glow of each new young leaf of green
And there in yon oaken tree sits the dove of love asinging
The meadows have sprung to life with buds of many colors
Soon the ewes will be lambing in the warming sun on high
My life will be filled with joy before this night is neigh.

Contemplation is a simple little thing
It makes one sit in wonder
At the thoughts that it does bring.
So sit in contemplation every chance you get
Your world will see a wondrous change
In the happiness that will be met.

William C. Moore, Jr.

Does the Soul Cry Out?

In Memory of Ruth Moore

When blue eyes have closed and the smile is no longer
To be seen on her tired wrinkled face.
When the body has withered and shrunken with no strength
Left to move at any pace.
Does the soul cry out to Almighty God
Please take me from this place?

The years had been long since the loss of her mate
A long and lonely thirty-year wait.
She kept up the struggle to live a good life,
But life isn't easy, always there's strife.
There are children to care for, fences to mend,
If only this loneliness would ever end.

Her memories are waves that wash in and out
Who are you people she often would shout.
The glow on her face when memories were clear
Would light up the room for everyone near.
She was grateful and loving for each passing day
I know she was special God made her that way.

The blue eyes are closed forever in sleep,
The smile is a memory forever to keep.
The body rest forever in peace,
But did the soul cry out to Almighty God
Please take me from this place?

AUTUMN LEAVES:

Dreams of Absurdity

Joey fell off the wagon and landed in a heap,
As I lay in my bed and drifted back to sleep.
Sister Margaret Mary prayed and began to weep
For poor Father Stephen who couldn't earn his keep.
Lay-a-bouts and drunkards are sleeping in the street
While ladies of the town are so often want to meet.
The sheriff and his deputies are making a big sweep
Forcing all the men to get back upon their feet.
Indians chasing cowboys who give up in defeat.
Big bears are now dancing to a rumba beat.
Across the watery purple sky a sailboat does streak
While little Mary Louise out her window she does peek.

From out the sodden cornfield, a booming sound is heard
I find myself saying this dream is just absurd.
Out in the barnyard, the cows have all conferred.
They have all agreed that the goats can't join the herd.
The cats and mice all squeaked and purred
That the dog's drunken barks all were slurred.
Papa saddled the horses when the strangest thing occurred
They said no coffee please, hot tea is much preferred.
All the chickens looked at the turkey saying he's a sad old bird
All he needs is a computer to make him a techno nerd.
To a noisy ringing, clanging in my dreams was I now stirred
My dreams all were gone and everything was blurred.

William C. Moore, Jr.

Enlightenment

Give away a smile each and every day
Change your outlook on life.
That is enlightenment.

Listen to the sound of one hand clapping
Or a tree falling in the forest.
That is enlightenment.

Hold back some words that would
Wound like a knife.
That is enlightenment.

Free up your mind, release trouble and strife,
Make peace with yourself.
That is enlightenment.

Look deep within the rocky stream
Remove the boulders, let the waters flow.
That is enlightenment.

Life is a gift to be lived with joy
Even death is a gift of release.
That is enlightenment.

There are many roads, paths and trails
On the trip to Illumination of the Spirit.
That is enlightenment.

Seek out the oneness with all things
For the core of all things is love.

AUTUMN LEAVES:

That is true enlightenment.

William C. Moore, Jr.

Eulogy to an Unknown Man

Here lies an unknown man, a brother, a son, a father.
Some of us might have known him, but most of us
Have never heard of him. We would have like him
And been proud to call him a friend, however,
Circumstances never gave us the opportunity to know
Him or his dreams.

There are no medals to decorate his chest. There are no
Public mourners who tear their clothes, wailing for his soul.
There is only this shell left behind after his soul's
metamorphosis
Which goes forward shining and bright into eternity. This
Remnant of his life will be put aside and scattered to the Four
Winds as if he had never been, nothing to show that he has
Passed this way.

Think of him occasionally as you move about your life.
Say a prayer that when our time comes we can
All meet again and get to know this friend
That we say farewell to this day.
We will raise our hands in salutes, our glasses
In cheer and our voices in song. The heavens
Will rock with laughter and joy will fall
Like a spring shower upon this earth

My friend, my brother, my son, go forward in peace.

Family Man

My father was a gentle man, a family man
Tall, lean and strong.
He never said, "It can't be done." He always said it can.
His guidance taught us right from wrong
His love taught us kindness
Against the prejudices of this world
He taught us color blindness.
"Be aware that every man was made in God's own image
And when you treat your brother wrong
It's God that you're offending."

Because my father was a family man
All things he took in stride.
Life's problems can't wear you down
If your family's by your side.
When I grew up and became a man
I walked with faith and pride.
It's up to you, my son; he said to be the best you can
I've taught you everything I know
There's not much more to teach you.
Now I hope that my life with pride will show
That I've become like him.

William C. Moore, Jr.

First Kiss, Last Memory

Memory flashes of when we met
This handsome man and I.
The thought of it still echoes in my mind's eye
And I never will forget.
He asked me to dance,
I gave him my hand
As they struck up the band
And all over the floor we did prance.

He held me tight as we danced under the lights
The night was filled with romance.
He was the one, I knew at a glance
Our meeting just seemed to be right.
It wasn't long before I had to go home
So I made my excuses to leave.
He followed me out and said, "I believe
That you shouldn't walk home alone."

We strolled down the lane
Under the huge August moon
And arrived at my door all too soon.
For out of the shadows love sprang
I gave him my key and he opened the door
I turned and whispered, "Goodnight."
He took my hand and under the light
Did kiss me and made my heart soar.

He walked slowly away into the night
I couldn't believe it was real.
This wonderful man with so much appeal,

AUTUMN LEAVES:

I had found my shining knight.
I pranced up the stairs and went to bed,
But we danced on and on all night.
With memories still warm, I arose at first light
Thoughts of him still filled my head.

That was fifty years ago, just a girl in my youth,
But I wouldn't have changed a thing
He gave me his love all bound in a ring
I knew that this man told the truth.
We lived long together through fair and foul weather
Our lives forever intertwined.
We've aged like fine wine
All because a dance brought us together.

William C. Moore, Jr.

Fishing with Dad

Bait, tackle and poles at the ready
An early four a.m. call
Sleep deprived and unsteady
For a cup of coffee I try to stall.

But Dad's eager and ready to go
"Come on now, we'll get coffee later.
Pick up the pace and don't be so slow."
If I changed my mind would I be a traitor?

On the road at last, it's already hot
A beautiful southern summer morning,
We're going to Dad's favorite fishing spot
Keep it a secret was his warning.

It's a two hour drive over a rough country road,
But we arrive at Eagle Lake intact
The silence is broken as we begin to unload
And the creatures begin to react.

We load up the boat and settle in
To paddle our way over the lake
Dad opens his pack and takes out a tin
Sprinkling the contents in our wake.

I don't know what was in that concoction,
But the smell was outrageously strong
Soon the water was boiling with great agitation
As around the boat the fish did throng.

AUTUMN LEAVES:

"That's just to let the fish know we're here
It would be wrong to take them that way."
We stopped near an old broken down pier
Now it was time to play.

We cast out our lines time after time,
But the fish kept slipping away
We continued our quest as the temperature climbed
The fish just stayed at bay.

At about one or two, we stopped for some food
Then decide to try once again
His line snagged on some willow wood
Creating a bit of a strain.

He cursed under his breath
Then his tackle he quickly reset
Now he would fight to the death
Declaring, "This game isn't over yet."

He cast out his line, this was the time
A big fish he was gong to catch
A nibble or two as he played out his line
He brought in a bass with a snatch.

The day had been fun for father and son
A memory of us playing together
The battle was fought and Dad had won
Just the two of us and beautiful weather.

William C. Moore, Jr.

Flapper

She's twenty-seven, beautiful and full of life
In two short years she'll be my father's wife.
Until then there will be time to dance
My father will provide the romance.
She already loves him, but there is no rush
All of his joking just makes her blush.

It's summer in the country and my father's come to call
All the family's there to meet him standing in the hall.
He's going to pop the question if he can get her all alone
He took her for a walk across the cobblestones.
Picking up the camera stopping by the truck
He had to have her picture to carry for good luck.

They walked passed the old red barn headed for the swing
He set her gently in the seat and pulled out a diamond ring.
"Will you marry me and be my wife
For the rest of our long life?"
She smiled her smile, lifting her blue eyes
Saying softly, "I know I've caught the prize."

AUTUMN LEAVES:

For Tom

I met you on a summer's night
We were young and filled with youthful vigor.
You made me laugh and we spent the night
Regaling each other with ribald stories of life.
What times we had in our carefree days of misspent youth,
Dinner parties, Sunday beer blast and bottles of wine.
We partied through our youth like a wastrel
Never seeing the end of the line.

Youthful adventures began to fade,
The joy no longer there.
Responsibilities, maturity, the standards of a man,
Pushed passed the party mentality to take us by the hand.
Success, money and big titles took on another light
Live life to the fullest, but work with all your might.
We buried ourselves in Fortune City,
A vast dark place without any pity.

All too soon we began to see
That kind of life wasn't for you and me.
Where was the joy? Where was the fun?
Get out of the darkness go into the sun.
We packed up our lives, let loose the debris,
Moved to the west with audacity.
The road that we chose to travel on
Led to the sea and Babylon.

Friends, games and good times abound
Laughter, music all around.
Party in a party town.

William C. Moore, Jr.

Travel here, travel there
Make no plans, go everywhere.
London, Paris, Milano, Venice, Vienna
Take a chance and be a winner.
Continental lovers, we.

We look back in wonder amazed at the view
To think that this life was meant for us two.
We've feasted and fasted, we've loved and we've cried,
But luck was with us as we stood side by side
Life wouldn't have been the thrill that it's been
Without each other from the start to the end.
The future's unknown, just a hazy view,
But know that for always there will be us two.

AUTUMN LEAVES:

For Trish: Let the Party Begin

Let the party begin, I'm free at last
Of the long years of loving you.
Of caring beyond all reasonable bounds
Of the jumping you put me through.

Let the part begin I'm free at last
Free to find someone new.
Someone who's eyes won't shine
The way that yours use to do.

Let the party begin I'm free at last
Free to go my own way.
To look for that someone who
Will make me want to stay.

Let the party begin I'm free at last
I've sent out the invitations
There'll be songs, there'll be dancing
Maybe some infatuations.

Let the party begin I'm free at last
What we had is but some dreams.
I won't be looking back for you,
But you'll be in my memories.

Love you always.

William C. Moore, Jr.

From Babylon-By-The-Sea

I think it's time to leave California and Babylon-By-The-Sea.
To find the trail that leads back in time, back to the other me.
I'm not afraid of the road less traveled or the dark wild lay of
The land, but somewhere back there on the map in my mind
Is the place where I want to be.

It's not so congested and the air is quite clean
There in this place in my mind.
The people are friendly and the streets aren't so mean
There life is gentle and kind.
In this place where I want to be.

I see all the buildings surrounding the square
The founder is standing with arms opened wide,
Welcoming you with warmth, peace and care
To come to his town and work side by side.
In this place where I want to be.

The sunsets are brilliant, the mornings are bright
The air is filled with perfume and song.
The birds and flowers are up at first light,
Peace and calmness last all day long.
In this place where I want to be.

Where is this place in my waking dream,
The place where I long to roam?
Where I can walk by the shimmering stream?
That place is still called home.

AUTUMN LEAVES:

Hath Thee No Love For Me, My Lady?

Hath thee no love for me, My Lady?
Of not my own accord didst I leave thee,
But by the king's own ill purpose.
Though far from thee and home was I
Thou wast always in my heart.
Hath thee no love for me, My Lady?
Hath thee no love?

Couldst I ever not have love for thee, My Lord?
By His Majesty's own hand didst he send thee away
Leaving my heart empty and forlorn.
Thou wast ever with me through my dreary days
And thou didst fill my dreams in slumber.
Couldst I ever not have love for thee, My Lord?
Couldst I ever not have love?

Canst we not live with love forever more together?
The king canst no longer send me away
For no longer doest he rule.
But thou, My Lady, have rule over my heart
And gladly will I surrender unto thee.
Canst we not live with love forever more together?
Canst we not live with love?

Wouldst I not welcome thee, My Lord, as ruler of my heart?
Thou will never be sent away from me
For all my life to thee I give the key.
Our lives are as intertwined as the white and red roses.
Surrender only thou the love still in thy heart.
Wouldst I not welcome thee, My Lord, as ruler of my heart?

William C. Moore, Jr.

Wouldst I not welcome thee?

I Beheld Thee in a Dream

In deep dark slumber thee came to me when I was but a youth,
Thy words spoke of the love we'd one day share.
Long have I waited for thee to come, the answer to my prayers.
At last thou are here and Aphrodite spoke the truth.
Thee looks at me with love, with longing and desire.
How can I not know that our love was meant to be?
Stay with me forever will always be my plea.
Thou are all that my heart and soul can aspire.
Come be my love and live with me in blessedness and peace.
Thou art the joy that fills my lonely soul.
Let us rejoice, our time has come to fill our lonely hearts.
Thou art here with me now all loneliness will cease.
Let our love make us whole.
Together forever now tagged by Cupid's dart.

William C. Moore, Jr.

I Sit In Contemplation

I sit in contemplation with thoughts
Running wild through my mind.
I slowly bring them under control
And think about loving you.

My surroundings fade as I see your face,
My arms reach out to you,
But time and distance has taken its toll
I'm left with empty space.

I wanted the world and everything in it,
You just wanted me in your life.
Too late I've learned I would have had it all
If I had made you my wife.

I watched you as you walked down the aisle,
Your smile never left your face.
I quietly left with a broken heart
To let you go on with your life.

You're married now with a family,
A husband, the luckiest man alive.
Two little girls as beautiful as you,
Your dreams have finally come true.

I sit in contemplation with thoughts
Running wild through my mind.
I sleep the sleep of an old man
Lost in my dreams about you.

AUTUMN LEAVES:

Morning

It's early Saturday morning and I wait
For the coffee to finish perking.
The light is subdued as the day
Lingers patiently for the sun to arise
Bringing warmth after the cold night.
TC bumps my leg letting me know
He's ready to go out for his first
Trip of the day.
Outside the air is fresh and clean.
The fragrance of jasmine fills the
Air mixed with the sweet cinnamon smell
Of wild alyssum.
TC hurries to do his morning inspection
To see what creatures has dared to
Set foot on his territory.
He flags a warning for all who would
Come back then runs to the front
To check out the neighborhood.
Sitting in the driveway, he looks up
The street taking note of a new car
Parked three houses up.
There's a light on in the house on
The corner where that crazy dog
Barks every time we walk by.
The house of his favorite lady
Is still dark and silent.
Checking to see if she's working
In her yard he wiggles and wags
His tail hoping she's there
So he can have a rough rub

From her talented hands. Alas,
She's not outside so he
Turns his attention to the side street
Where a cat sits lazily cleaning
It's fur safe and secure from his
Annoying charges.
A truck passes slowly by, the driver and TC
Each eyeing the other.
Down the street a car door slams,
He sits waiting for the engine noise,
But all is quiet, They must have
Changed their minds.
Inspection's over, he trots
Up the drive ready for breakfast.
The coffee's finished so I pour
Myself a cup, get TC his morning meal
And we settle down for a few silent
Moments before the day begins.

Autumn

William C. Moore, Jr.

It's Autumn

The winds have breathed a cooling word
And nature whispers a sigh of relief.
Gone are the harsh days of summer.

Coloring of trees has begun, it's Autumn.
God has taken His colorful brush,
To give the world vivid new
Colors for a short while.

Relish these day of gold , orange, yellow,
Red and green, for soon the branches
Will be bare and the snow will hide
The promise of tomorrow.

Collect the leaves like the child
You were, trying to save the
Memories of youthful Autumns of past years.

While other falls may come and go,
None will be better than this one,
Live it with adventure and joy, it's Autumn.

Like Sweet Love Always

Like the perfumed breezes that sweep across a tropical paradise
Like the gentle spring rains that fall on thirsty fields
Like the warm summer sun that heats the cool clean day
Like my love for you

Sweet as the nectar from the honeysuckle flower
Sweet as the honey from the comb
Sweet as the taste of a warm ripe peach
Sweet as my love for you

Love as soft as a baby's hair
Love as strong as Cupid's bow
Love as perfect as the golden sun
Love as beautiful as you

Always will you be in my dreams
Always will you be safe in my arms
Always will you know I'll be there
Always in love with you

William C. Moore, Jr.

Lines On A Map

Lines on a map leading away from home,
Songs on the radio about moving on.
Words in a letter from friends on the move
Staying behind how they all disapprove.

Dusty roads filled with dusty old cars
Heading out for the night to visit the bars.
Country dancing to hot western fiddles
Cowgirl constitute the eternal riddles.

Dreams cooling to the coyote's lonely howls,
Soft hooting from the old gray owl,
The quiet is broken as the back door slams
It's time for a walk with the dog and Grams.

Tomorrow the sun comes up once again
Words from an old song runs through my brain.
One day I'll pack up my bags and go moving on
One of the lines on a map leading away from home.

AUTUMN LEAVES:

Man and Hurricane

Eyes blazing with the light of a thousand fires
Defiant, hands ready to fight, they stand shouting,
"I will not give in."
These brave souls stand against the wind and sea.
As the hurricane moves ever closer, shouting,
"Get out of my way or you will die."
The town has been boarded up, shuttered like
An overused shipping crate, but of little protection
From the approaching storm.
This storm will destroy all thing in its path not
Caring about the outcome. Blind, mindless, unfeeling,
This raging wind and rain strikes out at anything
In its way, caring not what it shatters.
Building, homes or lives. Bent only on destruction
It sends debris flying, moving boats from the harbor
To the middle of town, wiping out lives like an
Angry child stomping on an anthill.
Those brave fighters who stayed behind
To fight the fight have lost before the match began.
Better to retreat with wounded pride than to lose your life
In a battle that no brave warrior can win.
Leave or be conquered and destroyed is the ultimatum.
Wisely, they choose retreat. Running with the wind pulling
Their hair and throwing obstacles in their paths.
Eyes still blazing they lift their voices shouting,
"I will not be subdued by you again. The next time
We meet I'll win."

William C. Moore, Jr.

Mankind

There is no tomorrow, only today.
Stars streak by in blurred lines
Illuminating nothing, but jagged memories
Of different times and different days
When the court jesters danced and pranced
Upon the world stage to entertain
The Kings of Self-Destruction.
While Beauty and Innocence were
Cast out into the dark cold world
On a trip of self-discovery.
Laughter echoes like thunder
And anger cries like a new born
Thrust out of its warm protected womb.
Angels look on in sadness
Determined not to interfere as man
Progresses up the ladder of life.
Better if man had stayed a beast
Than bring such hell into fruition.
Down corridors marked in bright colors
March the children of duplicity, lies and hate.
Through halls left dark,
Lit only by the candle of hope,
Move the offspring's of truth, justice and love.
Each bears witness to their
Rendition of "What's Best for Mankind."
No battle of swords, no loss of blood
Only loss of imagination and free will.
Mankind struggles for every gift of life
Then discards each one as if they had been
Given a stick. Ungrateful leading to uncaring

AUTUMN LEAVES:

Leads into isolation of all mankind.
God looks down on this puny world of war
Shedding a tear of disappointment that so great
A work has fallen into the abysmal pit of adversity.
Man cries out in fear, but is too proud to reach out a
Hand for help, instead he cries, "Abandon me not!"
Then refusing all efforts of rescue.
The future is now, so follow
The tiny flame of hope that it may cast
Out the darkness and free all life.

William C. Moore, Jr.

Missing You

You've gone away
But I had to stay
Now each lonely day
I'm missing you.

The old front porch swing
Where we use to sing
Has lost all its zing
It's missing you.

The blue skies are gray
Since you went away
And the sea hasn't much to say
They're missing you.

Birds refuse to sing
Even though it's spring
No music do they bring
They're missing you.

I only have one regret
Not being there when you left
I'll go through my life
Just missing you.

Mornings by the Sea

The light did sparkle on azure seas
As waves rolled in to the shore.
Birds flew high on ruffled wind
That blew against the cliffs.
Sand dunes sang one long clear note
In the early morning mist.
And yet my heart is lonely still
That beats within my breast.

The rain comes in from off the seas
To weep up on the shore.
Ships go by on bucking waves
To places that call my name.
Lighthouses sweep beyond the rocks
That wait beneath the waters.
And yet my voice is silent still
For no one is waiting there.

The land does tremble and falls away
And the sea moves closer to me.
Grasses grow on paths I've walked
Over seaside cliffs so tall.
How dark the day has just become
The clouds now hide the sun.
And yet my sight is steady still
To see another day.

The voice of life calls out my name
While I stumble through my days.
Spirits glide in a sea-fragrant breeze

William C. Moore, Jr.

As I start down the path for home.
Come back again they call to me
As they fade away from view.
And yet I have to walk from it all
For I cannot answer the call.

AUTUMN LEAVES:

My Beloved

Thy beauty is like the jeweled night skies
Glorious and shining in eternal night
With a touch of mystery in thine eyes
Thy lips are soft, sweet and filled with delight
Let my kisses fill thee with longing sighs
Bid me not to leave until first light

How sweet the perfume of thy breast
That intoxicates me, as doth a cup of ruby wine
Thy gentle passion doth my soul possess
I cannot be stilled 'til thou art mine
From my heart I thee address
Declare me now and I am thine

My Love

My Love, thou art more beautiful than the sun
That shines upon the new fallen snow
Thy name is as the sound of cymbals
That fills my heart with joy.
Thy burnish copper hair is as a halo
That surrounds thy glorious face.
Thy eyes are bluer than the bluest skies
Which cry out in jealousy.
Thy lips are as rubies that does beg to be kissed.
Thy voice is tender and filled with love
When thou speaketh to me.
Thy skin is soft, delicious to my tongue.
Round and full art thy breast that pillow my head.
Firm is thy belly that begs my kisses when I'm near to thee.
Thou art all that I desire.
Thou art all that I shall ever want.
Thou art my Alpha and Omega.

AUTUMN LEAVES:

New Orleans, The Queen City

New Orleans sits at the river's bend
The queen of the Mississippi.
She's a lady and she's a friend.
She's beautiful and she's a chippie
She's warm and she's cold,
But once you've felt her magic
You become one of her fold.

She's older than most cities
Though sometimes she's shabbily dressed
Not that she doesn't have pretties
She makes one think of Mae West.
A gourmand and a party hostess
She serves up all the best
Each year her party is the Mostess.

She's a lady with a past
She's a lady with a future
But she really can't be surpassed
She's a city full of adventure
You stay up late each night to please her
With Cafe au Lait and beignets
Until all time becomes a blur.

She'll let you go to move far away
But she never lets go of your heart
She knows that one has to stray
The city is really quite smart
You can travel the world
And have your adventures

William C. Moore, Jr.

But it's back to her arms that you're hurled.

The time coming soon, I can feel the old pull
I can hear the soft southern drawl
My dreams of being with her are full
Of hot summer nights that enthrall.
"Please wait for me for I'll be there soon
I promise to leave never again."
We'll be together forever under the big southern moon.

Ode to a Country Road

A red tail hawk silently surfs the air above you
Seeking a meal for its young.
Crows dart noisily out of the trees
Startled by the approach of a passing car.
Your long gray ribbon of asphalt winds lazily
Through the verdant wooded hills.
Weathered wooden houses, dulled and peeling,
Peek out from among the trees.
High upon a hill stand a bright red barn
Shelter for the horses nibbling grass in the pasture
Undisturbed by the rumbling on your hard gray surface.

Curving gently through the countryside
Like a snake let loose on a wet canvas.
Fording streams, gullies and chasms
Going ever onward toward the sea.
What will you do when at last you can go no further?
Sit gazing out to sea as the waves break
On the rock strewn shore and wait for the day to end?
When the sun dips below the darkened waters
The quiet settles in and under the starry night skies
New creatures cross your hard surface in search for food
While you expel your stored heat into the cooling darkness.

William C. Moore, Jr.

Ode to a Summer Morning

I watched the roses sway in the cool morning breeze.
As sparrows sit on the fence with ruffled feathers
That turn them into fluffy brown balls.
The morning sun with its muted rays of golden light
Create lacey patterns on the ground as it's filtered
Through the leaves of the oak trees.
How quiet is this morning.

From somewhere near by the sweet perfume of flowers
Drifted lazily in the breeze
If you listen closely, you can hear the rustle of some
Small creature as it scurries through the bushes.
Already the bees are up, humming as they go about
Their day, collecting essence from the many flowers.
How beautiful is this summer morning.

The path through the garden pulls me deeper
Towards the lily pond at its center.
Water bubbles softly from the mouths of stone frogs
That sit frozen at the four corners of the pool.
Koi swim slowly seeking the shade of the lily pads
As they playfully chase each other.
How joyful is this morning.

In quiet, shadowed solitude I sit, gazing at the wonders,
In a morning garden of perfect splendor.
I breathe the fragrance of exotic blooms
That fills the beds with riotous colors.
A tonic for the soul and spirit can be found
Where the finger of God has touched.

AUTUMN LEAVES:

How perfect is this morning.

Perchance We Should Meet Someday

You're dressed in silks and satins
And I'm dressed in a ragged coat.
Always before me like a standard
In a holy war, you go about your life.
We pass, but you never see me
I'm invisible to your eyes. There
Was a time not so long ago that I
Was just like you.
Life was filled with all its
Good bounty. I had a family and friends
And the money kept rolling in.
I had it all, but I wanted more,
More of everything.
My family left because I wasn't there.
My friends left because I didn't care.
My job went the way of an ill summer wind
And I was stranded with no where to sleep.
Tomorrow will be better. I'll bounce
Back to my former self, but things don't
Always have a happy ending.
The rest of the story I'll tell you
Perchance we should meet someday.

Playing Life's Game

Stumbling and falling as I move through life
I get up and try once again.
Life is a series of trials and errors
Not losing, but never winning.

With arms raised high in defiance
I shout out my rage at life.
"I may stumble and fall as I move about,
But I'll never give up trying."

Life awards me the brass ring for a while,
But all too soon my finger turns green.
I toss away this joke of life
As I prepare to fight once again.

I will not give up my struggle.
I will not fall prey to chance.
As long as I've breath in my body
I'll play life's game and I'll dance.

William C. Moore, Jr.

Sitting by the Ocean

With sun shining in clear blue sky
And a cool west wind a blowing
I make my way to a point up high
To watch the ships a going.

Gulls fly by on soft currents of air
Screeching and calling their mates
"Follow me if you dare."
As they sail out over the straits.

The ocean in its constant changing hues
As the waves move in and out
Make relaxing shades of greens and blues
Along the ridge top route.

The waves sing their siren's song
To all who comes their way
"Come to me and you'll belong,
Brother of the sea spray."

The sun dips down to cold blue waters
And the sea turns ruby red
But the songs go on from Neptune's daughters
As slowly the world goes to bed.

AUTUMN LEAVES:

The Ballad of Paris Parker

Paris Parker was his name
He stood about six foot four.
A big hulking log of a man
That filled the wide front door.
Long dark hair hung down his back,
His eyes were as dark as the night.
No man was foolish enough to attack
No man ever won a fight.

He pushed his way up to the bar
As the drinkers gave him room.
The dance hall patrons stared from afar
Some felt the cold hands of doom.
For Paris Parker had come to town
One thing that held no doubt
Tonight there would be a knock down
Tonight, a fighting bout.

Now Lovely Louise came out so sing
Her eyes and face did shine.
Her voice was soft like a breeze in spring
The song she sang so sublime.
She had him hooked with her first note
His eyes never left her face.
He watched the movement of her slender throat
As her song picked up its pace.

A man in love was Paris Parker
Nailed by a siren's song.
Lovely Louise was his heart's hijacker

And to him she would belong.
He made his move at her songs end
A gentleman he had become.
His love for her he would defend
To her he did succumb.

Now Danny Douglas had other plans
For he too was under her spell.
He was ready to post the wedding bans
And Paris Parker could go to hell.
A fight ensued and guns were drawn
As the patrons did take flight.
This was a test of blood and brawn
That lasted half the night.

One final lunge, they went for a gun
Two shots were heard outside.
Then came a scream from a mother's son
They knew someone had died.
As the patrons filed in about sunup
A terrible sight was seen.
The fight for love had drained the cup
And brought this painful scene.

There lay Paris Parker, as dead as a man could be,
Just a few feet away, Danny Douglas lay.
In the middle you see, in all that debris,
Lovely Louise had stepped in the way.
Three souls had that day been lost
For a beautiful girl so silky and soft.
Now forever lovers crossed
Their destiny had been bought.

AUTUMN LEAVES:

The Devil's Gold Mine

He came to the mountain all wet, tired and cold
For a pocket of gold, his soul would be sold.
At thirty-eight, he came from the east
This man they called John Franklin Makepeace.
Now years of gold panning had been lumbering along
He was just one more man in that gold seeking throng.

The winters were harsh, dark, cold and bleak
For long months on end the sun didn't peek.
He crawled up the mountain to stake out his claim
The fortune he sought was just a crap game.
Panning and mining, digging and blasting
The search for gold went on everlasting.

Day end and day out, he kept up his pace
The search for gold his soul did embrace.
But try as he might his luck just ran out
The mine went deeper, but no gold was about.
In anger and madness, he ranted and raved,
Where was the gold he so badly craved?

"I'll give you the gold, but there must be a trade."
Before very long a bargain was made.
A contract was drawn, in blood it was signed
And now to the devil his soul was resigned.
The snap of the fingers, smoke billowing about
A strike of the pick axe and gold nuggets fell out.

He couldn't stop digging to claim all his gold
Forever he'll mine there or so it's been told.

William C. Moore, Jr.

The sounds of the digging go on through the night
The curse of the gold bug has spread its blight.
One more man has now been assigned
To dig forever in the Devil's Gold Mine.

AUTUMN LEAVES:

The Journal

Yellowed roses turning to dust in a book of memories.
Letters written in perfect pen with I love you left unsaid.
Telephone calls went unanswered long into the night.
Words shouted in anger and the slamming of the doors.
Candlelit dinners to say I'm sorry and I apologize.

Memories from a lifetime of living and loving,
I read each dusty page seeing the images it creates,
Taking me back to times long forgotten and no more.
These precious scenes from someone's yesterday.

A box of books bought for naught at some yard sale,
There hidden among the dusty volumes lay the journal.
Unopened, unread and long forgotten by it writer
Yet kept because it held memories of youth.

Some pages blurred by tears recalling a lover's death,
Others brief and fill with anger over being left behind.
But life moves on and so must we,
A new lover's waiting just out of sight.

With babies, house and mortgage, it was the perfect life.
Children grow up and move away to start lives
Of their own. Then grandchildren and memories
Try to fill the waning days of winter's dim glow.

One light extinguished as one fades gently in the night,
Leaving behind a bright picture of yesterday's walk on earth.
With pen in trembling hand a few final words,
"Learn to love life and go home in peace."

William C. Moore, Jr.

The Killing of Rebecca

Silent voices that call in the night
To people no longer there.
Music plays in long empty rooms
As the dancers glide in silence.
Laughter echoes down dark dusty halls
Of lovers from yesterday.
The say the house is haunted
By the souls who came to stay.

Windows aglow in darkened rooms
Casting eerie scenes in the night.
Doors keep opening then slamming shut
As the spirits saunter about.
Whispers in the garden made by lovers
Meeting before they're found out.
Gunshots, screams and curses,
Weeping, begging pleas of mercy.

A statue by the pool in memory of Rebecca
Who died in the arms of her lover.
The shadow of the husband, who in jealous rage
Killed her, kneels weeping.
Each night the scene repeats itself
As the actors reprise their roles.
They will do so forever into eternity
Or so the story goes.

AUTUMN LEAVES:

The Sailor

When at last the sun has risen over yonder wooded hill,
While the land is washed in silence and all the world is still,
Comes riding on the seaward air the call of the seven seas.
The duffel has been mustered, adventures flies on the breeze.
Time has come to get the coat from the peg by the door
One last look around the room, then head out to the shore.

The tide is high, the ship slips away, the gulls headed out to sea.
How sweet it is on a sailing ship for now a man is free.
The ship dips low to the ocean floor, spray breaks over the bow.
Now sails fill out as we come about, through the waves we plow.
It weaves and bobs like a bottle cork afloat on a restless pond.
We ride it like a lizard clinging to an old palm frond.

Back on shore, a tear slides down, the face of one left behind.
Gone is her love, but still she wears two hearts intertwined.
As time goes on, the seasons change, one leading to the other.
The fire remains never growing cold, faithful to her lover.
Until that bonny sunny day there are sails upon the bay
The sweetest joy of all is her sailor is home to stay.

William C. Moore, Jr.

The Visit

With shaking hands, I rang the bell
On a dark and blustery night.
I'd come to tell all farewell
And I was feeling quite contrite.

The door creaked open just a crack
A sliver of light escaped.
Two dark brown eyes stood looking back
In a body of unfathomable shape.

"I beg your pardon for calling so late,
But the family I really must see."
A screech came from the old front gate
Like the cry of a forlorn Banshee.

As the door opened wide I peered inside
Wondering just where they could be.
Where in the old house did they reside
Looking around I couldn't see.

"Come this way, sir." he said to me
In a voice as deep as a grave.
It was no request, but seemed more of a decree.
By now I wasn't so brave.

"Don't wake them up if they're asleep
I can wait until tomorrow."
On the walls our shadows slowly creep
Filling me with deep tearful sorrow.

AUTUMN LEAVES:

"I'm sure they would want to see you
They don't get many guest of late."
As I walked on my deep fear grew
By now I was in quite a state.

He stops at a door, opposite the head of a boar,
Three times he knocks on the wood
A muffled, "Come in." was heard through the door
I wasn't so sure that I should.

But I stepped inside as the door opened wide
"Come in, come in." I heard once again
Suddenly she's standing at my side
And then hits my foot with her cane.

"We must have a drink. What do you think?"
What else could I do but agree?
"You pour us a drink," she said with a wink
"I'll have a glass of Chablis."

The old man sat in the fire's glow
Taking in this merry scene.
"What are you doing here?" he wanted to know
The question wasn't said to be mean.

"I've come to say I'm going away,
But I'll be back in a couple of weeks."
A smile on his lips in a moment of play
Brought color to his cheeks.

"Now do take care and be aware
That everything will be all right."
"You go have fun and we'll say a prayer

William C. Moore, Jr.

That your trip will be a delight."

I kissed them both, grabbed for my coat
As I made my way to the door.
"I'll give you a call and drop you a note."
And left the parents that I adore.

AUTUMN LEAVES:

The Whispering Winds

The whispering winds keep calling my name
And I feel I should be going, but a gentle tie
Binds me here and my life is not a game.
I want to follow the birds as they fly
Over mountain meadows and glacial lakes,
Through valleys deep and hidden,
Through hellish sleet and soft snow flakes,
As they do their inner bidding.
But that gentle tie that holds me here
Is one that can't be broken.
Within my heart, my strength, I fear
Isn't just there as a token.
People, places and things do bind
With soft chains to the heart.
Were I a cold man that was so blind
I would not be so faint to start.
But the whispering winds keep calling my name
And there's a tugging at my other self
A call to which I cannot lay claim.
The whispering say to free thyself
Come move with me across this land
And behold what I have seen.
From the frozen tips of Iceland
To places you have yet to dream.
I whisper back that I can't go
For my promise has been made,
But come again in winter's snow
When the cold has long overstayed.

William C. Moore, Jr.

The Writer's Struggle

Give rise to words yet unspoken
Praise thoughts that are yet to come,
Stand tall and straight to meet your fate
With a sheaf of paper, a writing pen
And a bottle of ink to dip it in.
Let words flow like droplets of tears
To cover each hard earned page.
Write 'til your fingers ache and
Words no longer come, then set it
Aside and wait for a while to let
Each line ripen.
Take up your pen and read it again
Expunge the over ripe words.
Be bold, hard and strike out the lines
That belong in another verse.
Set it aside and go on your way
Come back and read it another day.
Look hard and long at this poet's song
And rewrite it once again.
It the muse be true you will be through
And the page a work of art.

AUTUMN LEAVES:

Tread Carefully, O Man

Tread carefully, O Man, upon this land
Lest you leave your footsteps behind
Where tomorrow's child must make amends
For the follies of mankind.

Tread carefully, O Man, protectors of this land
Your actions should be with forethought
Or the world you leave to tomorrow's child
Will all be for naught.

Listen carefully, O Man, to Nature's cries
Her pleas shouldn't fall on deaf ears
The actions on all fragile life today
Will result in tomorrow's tears.

Live respectfully, O Man, with life's diversity
Let no one thing be above the rest
Neither man or beast on land or sea
Is worth the acid test.

William C. Moore, Jr.

Upon Leaving the Company of Friends

We said goodnight and I walked away
Feeling lost in the dark empty streets.
Without their friendship the night grew colder
Like a walk on an artic ice flow.
Their joy of life buoyed my sagging spirits
As we danced our way through city streets
Celebrating life, love and youthful freedom.
Joyful youth, how soon you're left behind.
Forgotten, yet are memories stuffed in a box
Of yesterday's leftovers to be remembered
In old age when one wistfully looks back
At roads taken and choices made.
Sweet friends of the Night, stay and dance
One more dance before the day
Peeks from the star embroidered covers of night.
Let us raise high our glasses in friendship
And seal our promise of forever.

AUTUMN LEAVES:

Windows

Windows looking out from stony face houses
Like strange eyes viewing the world.
Some are blind with curtains drawn tight,
While others sleep with shades down halfway.
What do they think about all through the day
As they watch the world slowly drift by?

Like some multi-eyed bug, the hotel sits gazing
With a three hundred-sixty degree view.
Does one side like what it sees better than the other
Or is it all the same to its brain?
Can they see a friendly face that returns time after time?
Perhaps, it's all ants at a picnic.

Some look out on the world with multi-colored eyes.
Framed by their maker in lacey patterns
To reflect the beauty deep within
By a bright and warming sun.
There are those that look up with views of blue,
Blue skies and stars that light up the night.

Big and tall, short and small, as varied
as mankind. Window see, but never
Tell the secrets of the world.
Polished and clean, dull and dusty,
A reflection of a state of health,
A reflection of the man within.

William C. Moore, Jr.

You Can't Hold Me Back

You can't hold me back
Though my youth is filled with indecision.
You can't hold me back
Because all others have doubts
For my spirit will support me.

You can't hold me back
Though life's roads are strewn with strife.
You can't hold me back
When dreams have crumbled to dust
For I will not accept defeat.

You can't hold me back
Though you talk words of defeat.
You can't hold me back
Because it hasn't been done
For I'm a pioneer of life.

You can't hold me back
Though I'm long in tooth and gray.
You can't hold me back
Even if life seems to have passed me by
For I will not put down my sword.

You can't hold me back
Though toilsome may be the task.
You can't hold me back
With doubt and confusion
For my future is written in the stars.

AUTUMN LEAVES:

Speak to me in words of strength
Tell me you believe in what I can do
To light the path for others to follow
Because you can't hold me back.

Winter

Awakening to a New Day

Light has broken through my chamber window
Turning the darkness into a patchwork display.
Dreams are hiding in the darkest corners
Only to be destroyed as the day grows brighter.
The birds are up and singing a cheery, "Good Morning."
To all creatures of the world.
While the fountain in the yard next door gurgles
With a more vibrant note, welcoming the bright new day.
I lay quietly breathing the fresh cool air as I
Slowly chase my sleep drugged mind to a more wakeful state.
Coffee's perking, I can hear its bubbling laughter
Soon the aroma will drift back to me
Enticing me to leave my warm lair to
Partake of some of its dark flavorful brew.
One sip will wash away all remnants of
Last nights dreams leaving the stark reality of day.
What has to be done today? Where do I have to go?
The planning has started and the mind is in gear
Life's little journey is about to begin.
"God, let me use this day wisely." I pray.

Birthday Boy

The cake has been baked and covered in frosting.
The presents lie hidden in the dark.
Tonight is the time for celebrating
For he's reached his three quarter mark.
With champagne, wine and good food
We'll toast the night away in a joyful mood.

One more year of victory at the gate,
Another year of wisdom to share.
We'll stay awake and party late,
But he falls asleep in his chair.
Just let him sleep, the party will keep
Let him have his little cat nap sleep.

He awakens refreshed, has a good stretch.
Now the time has come for some fun.
So it's off for the birthday gifts to fetch.
A loving cup to the "Old Fishing Bum,"
A music box for him to enjoy
That plays sweet "Danny Boy."

There's laughter, there's jokes, some wonderful folks
All here to give him good cheer.
We tell anecdotes, have a few quotes
About life and having no fear.
But all things must end, it's now nearly ten
Let's do it again next year.

Capturing the Moment

I wander the hills and mountainsides
Searching for adventures,
A wall to climb, a trail to hike,
A picture to capture on film.
Animals go before me like the parting of the seas,
But always, always beyond the line of sight.
At times I'm lost, completely in the moment,
Overwhelmed by the sights and sounds
That surround me in the beauty of nature.
At mountain crest, I look to the west
To the deep cerulean sea
Going on forever to meet the sky
At some distant point in the future.
Gulls sail silently above the dark blue waters
Riding on waves of warm air
Like surfers on their surf boards.
Occasionally a boat or ship is seen
Far out on the horizon,
Plowing its way through rolling waves
Going ever forward to some unknown destination.
I sit and drink in the moment
The camera at my side.
How do you capture feelings on film?
How do you even try?
I click the shutter in my mind
And capture it forever.

AUTUMN LEAVES:

Choices, Paths and Trails

Don't talk to me of things I should do
Or of things that will bring me regret.
Tell me about the joys of this life
Of goals, of honors I should pursue.
And when I'm down, tired of the struggle,
Just making it day by day,
Talk to me of what I have learned
Not what I've tossed away.

Life's lessons are choices, freely given,
With many paths and many trails.
Don't sit back waiting for life to happen,
Get out and meet it each day.
Take a chance on the path least chosen,
Learn something new along the way.
Seek out a new friend from a different path,
Seek out a different point of view.
Don't just let life happen, let it happen anew.

Honors and glory are all slight of hand
They're here and then they're gone.
But the lesson that comes from what you can learn
Will stay with you all of your days.
Find joy in your life, along with the strife.
Take pride in a job well done.
Each different path taken is a new trail to travel,
A different view of the world,
Opens your eyes to tomorrow.

Don't close your mind 'til you close your eyes

William C. Moore, Jr.

Live a life that is open to all things
All things are open to you.
Make your own magic, it's there in your mind,
Life's whatever you want it to be.
Choices are never wasted, they're just another chance
To learn a new way to smile, to learn a new way to see.
Wake up tomorrow determined to change
Take a chance, go out and play in the rain.

Daffodil Hill

The old house, long since gone,
That once had crowned the hill
It now sings a springtime song
Of yellow daffodils.

A lonely chimney stand watch each day,
A sentry on the hill.
But happy little daffodils go up to play
As all around yellow blossoms do spill.

Long winters covered a promise of spring
Slowly about the hill the blossoms rise
A crown of gold they did bring
And surprised delight to human eyes.

William C. Moore, Jr.

Dare To Be

When life seems stale and boring
Dare to be wild and free.
When friends let you down and can't be found
Dare to be forgiving and kind.
When your mind says, "You can't do that."
Dare to shout, "Yes, I can."
Set yourself free and just dare to be.

When things go awry and all seems bleak
Dare to take it in stride.
When the sky is dark and full of tears
Dare to dance in the rain.
When you're all alone with no one to phone
Dare to make time for yourself.
Set yourself free and just dare to be.

When life is a jumble and you're on the run
Dare to slow down and breathe.
When time is short and a job's half through
Dare to ask someone for help.
When your friends want to party and dance
Dare to let go of your worries and woes.
Set yourself free and just dare to be.

Don't live for the future, it may never come.
Don't live in the past, it's over and done.
Stay in the present that's all you can see.
This is your moment, now dare to be.

Day Has Gently Closed the Door

Day has gently closed the door,
As night draws the curtains.
A hush has fallen over all
As life has put down its burdens.
The cat has eaten, the night now calls.
The dog at his sentry post, hear him snore.

Rummaging once again in pleasant memories
Chasing sleep away with thoughts of yesterday.
 It was springtime, no, it was summer,
Or was it just a late seasonal dogday
When we marched to a different drummer?
How brave we were with all our certainties.

Clouds covered the horizon, blocking out the sun.
We wanted justice, we fought for equality,
We sought out love and pushed out hate.
We stood together for accountability
Before it was too late.
The war of our generation had to be won.

Sleep had edged a little closer, images begin to fade.
Where was I? I don't remember.
The night was cold, I held her close
It must have been December.
How beautiful was my Rose.
To keep her ever true to me I gave her a ring of jade.

Before too long my Rose was gone
The way of the lover's world.

William C. Moore, Jr.

She broke my heart never looking back
My dreams had become unfurled
And as dark as the night was black.
I stifled another yawn.

Gently sleep encompasses my mind
Softly closing doors to yesterday.
One last glimpse of Rose, one quick look back,
Now sleep was on its way.
The body relaxes and the mind goes slack
All dreamy thoughts get left behind.

AUTUMN LEAVES:

For Winter is Drawing Neigh

The autumn air is crisp and clean
For winter is drawing neigh
Soon snow flakes will paint all
In a soft white blanket, hiding
Imperfections in a beautiful painting.
But life will sleep through winter's long night
Waiting for the alarm in spring.

Leaves are now glowing in vivid colors
For winter is drawing neigh.
Bare branches filling the forest
Like skeletal hands reaching toward heaven.
Furry creatures will scurry up bare tree trunks
To play tag on the branches
While surrounded by soft while silence.

Soft tap, tap taps in the wooded hills
For winter is drawing neigh.
The gatherers have come to collect the sap
To cook on a cold winter's day.
With buckets full of maple nectar
They hurry back to their farms
As another gathering season is marked well done.

The pumpkins and corn are brought in from the fields
For winter is drawing neigh.
Jack O lanterns walk the night of ghosts and goblins
While pumpkin pies bake slowly in the oven,
Their aroma filling the house.
Friends and family join together in a feast

William C. Moore, Jr.

Thankful for another year.

Home to Bellevue

My bags are packed and waiting
The taxi's at the door,
For months I've been debating
What am I leaving for?

In nightly dreams I hear the call
Bellevue wants me home.
The magic of it does enthrall
No more will I roam.

I feel the enchantment calling me
Jasmine fills the air.
It will be day of jubilee
Because my heart is there.

William C. Moore, Jr.

Images of Life

A flash of forest, a glimpse of the sea,
The sound of a woodpecker hollowing a tree,
Mixed fragrances of flowers,
A cold winter's day slow passage of hours
These are the images of life.

A voice softly speaking, a caressing touch,
The face of the person you love so much,
A baby's gurgle as it's put down to bed,
The soft fuzzy hair that covers its head.
These are the images of life.

The birthdays, Christmas and holiday lights,
A family gathered to celebrate the night.
The gifts to be opened are stacked all around
A disappointed child is not to be found.
These are the images of life.

The loss of a parent, may they rest in peace,
A long sorrowful journey back to the east.
The clouds are all weeping and the trees are all bare
A small white church just waiting there.
These are the images of life.

The springs and summers, winters and falls,
Old age has come and you've done it all.
The paths have been walked and bridges all crossed
Just look back at life and don't count the loss.
These are the images of life.

Judgment Day

When at last these days are done
And our good deeds are counted one by one
Where will we stand on Judgment Day?
Will we go forth or be sent away?

Did we do all that we could
To be of help and do some good?
Did some of our good deeds go astray
When help was needed did we turn away?

Will on that day we be called to task
and have our failures be unmasked?
Will we hear the final decree
Away from here, you didn't see?

Where will we stand on Judgment Day?
Did we work or did we just play?
Out of love, did we pray
Lord, let me be with You on Judgment day.

William C. Moore, Jr.

Make Gentle the Ride Across the River

Make gentle the ride across the river
Then lay me down on a grassy slope.
Let not the cold be cause to shiver
But let me kiss the sun of hope.

Let the angels take me by the hand
And lead me out into the light
Walk me safely pass the strand
Away from darkness and the night.

Greet me as a long lost friend
Be not afraid and let me sing
Of my life until the end
Then let the bell of death to swing.

Perchance we will live anew
Perchance our lives will intertwine
When once again we must review
And see our lives with eyes un-blind.

Walk softly pass my shadowed box
But shed not tears for me
For tears will rust the best of locks
Just remember I'm now free.

Make gentle the ride across the river
Then lay me down on a grassy slope
Let me face the rising light at dawning
To kiss the sun that gave me hope.

AUTUMN LEAVES:

Memories

My memories of Elizabeth, written late in the night,
Even as she lies sleeping next to me.
Maybe she dreams of younger days with
Other friends and other lovers
Racing with her over the sandy beach
In cold, clammy and wet clothes.
Elizabeth and evenings filled with laughter and wine. Me
Standing beside her on our wedding day.

William C. Moore, Jr.

Memories of an Icy Winter

The cold, cold wind blew out of the north
Settling in the sunny south.
No slow transforming of gentle autumn colors,
Leaves suddenly going from green to black overnight
Falling from branches left bare for the first time in their lives.
Winter lingered about with wicked winds,
Dropping temperatures, turning puddles
Into small skating rinks,
Gifts to all children brave enough to accept them.
A winter rain came late one night,
Coating everything in glimmering ice,
Icicles formed along rooflines giving
The scene a Currier and Ives look.
Trees coated in ice, popped and cracked,
Crying for relief,
As the weight bowed low the branches.
Power lines crept dangerously down,
Sagging in their icy coats.
No school today, no cars can travel
Upon the black iced roads.
For five long days life came to a halt,
Covered in ice, hiding from the sun.
Then overnight the cold retreated
Beaten back by the warming rays.
Mothers sighed in great relief, children cried
In anticipation of catch up days at school.
Fathers, who had worked through it all,
Said a pray, grateful that the storm was over.
The air was filled with drip, drip, drip,
As slowly, the hand of ice relinquished its grip.

AUTUMN LEAVES:

Each drop a note in a springtime symphony
Seldom heard this far south.
Streams began to gurgle and laugh as the runoff
Of melting ice bubbled over the rocks adding
Their notes to nature's music.
Birds, quiet since the stormy first day,
Now sang a chorus in protest of winter's bleakness.
Life had returned to earth's frigid body
Resurrected from those cold dark days.

William C. Moore, Jr.

Missing Yesterday

I miss my yesterdays and all my friends,
The parties, the laughs and good times.
Had time but told me how soon they'd be gone
I would have held them a little closer.
When I was young and dancing away the night
Tomorrow never crossed my mind.
Friends can in and out my doors like
The turnstiles in a subway. Leaving a few
Memories to be pressed between the pages
Of a dusty book and the question, "I wonder
Where they are today?"
Some I will meet on a different path
That I have yet to take, others will sit
And wonder, like me, about yesterday.
It's understood we can't sit still, life
Doesn't work that way, but the friends
Who touched my very soul should never
Be allowed to stray. Friends aren't cheap,
They don't come by the dozen. I can't
Just toss them away, so why have so many
Been left by the side like toys when a
Child's finished play. Where are they now?
Do they remember all the fun and good times
We had? All the tears shed when we were sad?
I can treasure each memory, each youthful face,
All the times we were together and bind them
All in a golden book and mark on the cover,
Forever.

AUTUMN LEAVES:

Musings on a Lifetime

Photographs, souvenirs and memories of youth
Casting shadows over dreams of a lifetime.
Dancing in the moonlight, laughing in the sun,
Walking in the rains through trails among the oaks.
Football games, sock hops and a cherry red Chevy
Life was easy and we were so cool.
Parking at the lakefront and talking through the night.
Jealousy and breakups, tears and regrets,
Love won and lost. How brief the span of time.

College halls, new friends, new life has begun.
Laughter echoes in silent hallways.
Library dates, study through the nights.
New loves come and old loves fade
Welcomed holidays, weekend plans to get away,
Celebrations as semesters come and go.
Graduation springs forth in joyful anticipation.
A proposal, acceptance and the planning begins.
Enter the old boyfriend, exit the plans.

Rock and roll, hippies and free love, so cool,
So solid, man. Coffee houses with beat poetry,
Artist painting in the lofts, writers down the hall,
A clarinet weeps from the fire escape and
The wine goes from hand to hand. Pass around the joint
As the room slowly fills with smoke. No escaping
From the tranquil dreams that laid bare the souls of youth.
Stumble down the hallway, take care going down the stairs,
Escape before it's too late, go now before you wake.

William C. Moore, Jr.

The business world calls your name, come and join your peers.
Title, money and long, long hours fill year after weary year.
How long the life that has no joy, how sad the bitter soul.
The young man cries, the old man dies of tears he cannot shed.
For twenty years of constant toil, the flame of life grows shorter
But dreams of love still linger on the backdrop of the mind.
It's time to put away the work; it's time to move life forward.
Let loose the shackles that bind you to a dull and boring world
Time to fan the flames to wake this sad existence.

How mellow lay the middle years that I had carved with joy.
Everyday the sun did shine behind the clouds of gray.
The value of friendships grew, more valuable than gold.
As family, friends and lovers clung like sweet jasmine
Outside the window on hot summer full moon nights.
Tears were shed for those who could stay no longer
For their mission here was over and their peace had been won.
Remember all the good times, say a prayer and have a drink
And let a smile be in its place as a breeze does kiss you face.

AUTUMN LEAVES:

Night

The sun has long sank beneath the waves
Fog had drifted silently over the land
While in homes TV's blare out commercials and
Programs that put the masses to sleep.
Night, wonderful night, once again has come.
Quiet has settled on our world by the sea.
Restless waves wash the shore
Leaving silver traces upon the black sand.
The temperature drops cooling down
This sun washed piece of paradise.
Night in all it mystery and glory lies on
This tiny segment of earth like
The warm embrace of an old lover.
Slowly and softly is she wooed and seduced,
The before she has awakened, night leaves.
On the bedside table, a note,
A quick one word, left for her to find.
It reads, Tomorrow.

William C. Moore, Jr.

Old Age and I

We sit side by side, Old Age and I
As alike as two peas in a pod.
I think of a memory and Old Age will sigh
And close his eyes with a nod.
This goes on all day as Old age has a way
Of making you feel quite odd.

Do you remember our first girlfriend?
Do you remember our very first dance?
The love affairs we had to defend
In those days of love and romance.
I wake Old Age up and as him again,
Do you remember our first love?

Days will go by when Old Age just sleeps
Beside me in our comfortable chair,
And then there are day when he just weeps
Yes, Old Age and I are quite a pair.
Memories sweet are ours to keep
But just ask us and we'll share.

AUTUMN LEAVES:

Old Age and Memories

A friend came calling yesterday
One that I hadn't seen for years.
We talked of old times when we were young
And what we've been doing of late.
Tea was served on the veranda
As we sat warming in the sun.
It was a lovely visit from someone I loved
Another treasure for my memory.

The nurse looked on shaking her head,
"Poor dear, I wonder who she's talking to this time?"
You see, no one comes calling anymore
She's outlived all of them,
But still she struggles on.
Lines sometimes blur between the years
Making yesterday today.
Youth is in bloom again and life is good.

There are day when life is crystal clear
When her eyes stay filled with tears.
She wonders why life is so long
And why death has not yet appeared.
Age is not a pretty thing that everyone admires
Even wisdom and mature beauty can last too long
When she has trouble recalling the past year.
Then she drifts off into fitful dreams.

Do the loves of her life come calling
When she's sitting all alone?
Is this some chemical imbalance from

William C. Moore, Jr.

A dark part of her brain?
Perhaps it's one of these that
Gives her doctors' fear.
Could it be that those who have passed on
Are really truly here?

Because no one else can see them
Do they not exist?
Is this the sound of one hand clapping?
So far away yet so near.
She doesn't care nor does she fear
The images that she sees.
She's not alone, family is all around
Keeping watch over her always.

On the Way to Eternity

If one glittering drip of rain was a minute of time
Then a puddle would be a day of laughter.
A rill would be a week of dreams,
And a creek would be a month of hopes
All flowing towards the sea.
The rivers would be a lifetime of love
Moving ever forward to the ocean of eternity.

If one perfect drop of rain was a day in a lifetime
Then a puddle would be a week of hope and youth,
And a rill would be a month of love and joy.
The sinuous creek would be a year of perfect happiness
Made for you and I.
The rivers would be a lifetime we spent together
On the way to eternity.

If this crystal drop of rain was a whispered, "I love you."
Then a puddle would be my warm embrace.
A rill would be all my memories of living each day with you.
The swift flowing creek would spill over its banks
With the love I have for you.
The rivers would be our lifetime together
As we move toward eternity.

William C. Moore, Jr.

Reflections on Aging

When days grow long and the body tires
Of the stress we put it through.
Tired of other peoples wants and desires
And your mood is deep dark blue,
Sit yourself down in your easy chair
Put up your feet and sigh
Just close your eyes and whisper a prayer
To the Lord up in the sky.

When nights grow cold and the body's old
and you life is filled with moans and pains.
When you feel like you life has just been sold
And you're shackled with rusty chains.
Take a walk down to the soft sandy beach
Watch the moon surf on the waves.
Listen closely to the moonlight speech
That's whispered in the caves.

When sight grows dim and shadows abound
On the brightest of sunny days,
When the hearing fails and there is no sound
Remember the wild days of youth that set you ablaze.
In wastrel young dreams of childhood yearnings,
The bands, the nights of rock and roll, dance halls
Struck down by futility, went back to learning.
Until enclosed by maturity's walls.

Memories can fade or sharpen with age
And with respect some are best forgotten.
There are two life choices you can make, rage,

AUTUMN LEAVES:

That will leave you as a man misbegotten,
Or the sage, at peace with the world and himself.
Let the world see you as a light to follow
A great book pulled down from the shelf
Then life's not such bad medicine to swallow.

So Soft the Winds of Yesterday

So soft the winds of yesterday
When all the world was young.
The golden glow of youth, my child,
Was a prize we thought we had won.
Youth gave rise to illusions of eternity
Like a flag carried forth in the wind.
Around the Bacchanal feast we did gather
To waste away our days in drunken pleasures
While life with all its gloried treasures
Just hung her head and cried.

So harsh the breeze of tomorrow blows
How cold to these ancient bones.
The warm tales of age, my child,
To your ears are just a drone.
Wisdom grows or so I'm told
In proximity to ones age,
But still the tales that would be told
Will soon forgotten be.
The adventurers of a long, long life
Shall hang their heads and sigh.

The Path of Life

The Path of Life is paved with stones
Hewn from tears and sorrows.
Each one is labeled by the trials
Of the one that walks upon them.
Some walk slowly as they go through life,
Weighed down by cares and troubles.
Others march gaily forward to different
Beating drums and the clacking of castanets.
There are those that dance and skip along
Barely touching the path at all.
Most walk carefully along life's path
Placing each foot firmly down
Before they scout the ground ahead
Lest a pebble blocks their way.
I say walk the path with joy and hope
As it wanders through dark forests
And over flowering dales.
Each curve, each step, will lead you home
If you see beauty everywhere.
Take time to enjoy the walk,
Take time to smell the flowers,
For all too soon the path will end
Perhaps around yon bend.

William C. Moore, Jr.

The Snows of Yesteryear

I remember the snows of yesteryear
When the world and I were young.
Clean and fresh without a care
Life had just begun.
I hopped, skipped and danced my way
Through all of life's trials and test
Until at last the time ran out
I became like all the rest.
Away went all my childish dreams
As leaves down the Avenue of Time.
The winds of change blew all away
But not the words of my mind.
Hold tight lest they drift afar
Down some dark forbidden highway
Where mortals fear the wrath of gods
On every street and byway.
I locked them tight and hid the key
Where no man alive could ever steal.
My future life I planned with care
With myself I mad a deal.
I never thought it would take so long
To find that small golden key.
I searched high and low, inside and out,
When at last it came to me.
Believe in yourself in whatever you do
Know that your answers are there.
Let yourself be strong and true
But do it with loving care.

Then The Winter Came

I remember how colorful the forests were
And then the winter came.
Silent and softly snow drifted down
Dusting the trees in coats of white.

The meadows lay deep under the blanket
White, cold, undisturbed and unblemished.
No trails from animals seeking shelter
In the forest under the snow laden trees.

Winter sun soon will melt the dusty covering
Sending droplets of water cascading below
On to the animals congregated to stay warm
In the frigid temperatures of Arctic winds.

For months the forests will be hidden in white coats
But life is always there, hiding in and under
Each snow covered bush and hilltop
Waiting for the kiss of spring to awaken.

William C. Moore, Jr.

Thoughts on a Foggy Day

The fog is on the move again
Silently, softly, unhesitatingly.
Gray fingers reaching inland
Grasping, clutching, covering.
Until all sounds are muffled and
The world is hushed, peaceful.
Slowly the fog thickens, blanketing
Everything as it moves carefully
Over the seaside community graying
Out all vision to the outside.
Life is as it was before birth
Warm, safe and comfortable.
Nothing exists beyond the window,
As the world stays locked in quiet
Desensitizing gray fog until once
Again all is lifted and life begins anew.

To Hear the Wild Birds Sing

Be still and hear the wild birds sing
A song of joy and thanksgiving.
All through the forest the chorus does ring
It's a wonderful way of living.
Let loose the songs of praise to God above
From every creature here below.
As all life was created in love
And praise to God we all must show.

When Judging Others

It's a man's heart that must be judged
The center of our All.
After we've walked where the others have trudged
We can understand their fall.

Perhaps when judging yesterday
Critics of life might recall
Man's actions go every which way
As they did before the fall.

One man sings a song of joy
While another will cringe in despair.
The first will spend his days as a boy
The others just sits in his chair.

Along life's path, disguised as truth, lie
Pain, anger and frustration.
Just be careful what truth you buy
For it can destroy your inspiration.

Make peace with yourself along the way,
Show kindness to all those you meet.
Find a place in your life for some to stay
Friends are never obsolete.

Don't spend your life judging others,
Accept them as they are.
Under our skins we all are brothers
On our way beyond the stars.

About the Author

William C. Moore, Jr. is the author of numerous poems published in various anthologies. He has a chapter of poems in ELDER TREE VOICES by the Senior Coastsiders of Half Moon Bay, California published by Lulu. Com. He is retired and living in Mandeville, Louisiana.